Insights In-Between

Insights In-Between

A Ministry Student's Perspective on Youth Ministry

JACOB WINN

RESOURCE *Publications* • Eugene, Oregon

INSIGHTS IN-BETWEEN
A Ministry Student's Perspective on Youth Ministry

Copyright © 2019 Jacob Winn. All rights reserved. Except for brief quotations in critical publications or reviews, no part of this book may be reproduced in any manner without prior written permission from the publisher. Write: Permissions, Wipf and Stock Publishers, 199 W. 8th Ave., Suite 3, Eugene, OR 97401.

Resource Publications
An Imprint of Wipf and Stock Publishers
199 W. 8th Ave., Suite 3
Eugene, OR 97401

www.wipfandstock.com

PAPERBACK ISBN: 978-1-5326-7188-3
HARDCOVER ISBN: 978-1-5326-7189-0
EBOOK ISBN: 978-1-5326-7190-6

Manufactured in the U.S.A.   JANUARY 9, 2019

Contents

Acknowledgements | vii

Introduction | ix

1. When the "Bad Kids" Get Marginalized | 1
2. The Union of Optimism and Honesty | 6
3. Striving to be Peacemakers | 11
4. Encouraging Curiosity | 15
5. Eccentricities are Blessings | 19
6. Compassionate Actions | 24
7. The Voices of Our Youth | 28
8. Hellfire | 32
9. Christians and Nature | 36
10. Collective Sin | 40
11. Exploring Scripture Boldly | 45
12. Love and Obedience | 50
13. Christ's Love on Display | 55
14. Passion for Our Calling | 59

Appendix | 63

Acknowledgements

I would like to thank Wipf & Stock, specifically Matthew Wimer, Daniel Lanning, and everyone else who has helped make this book come to be.

I would also like to thank all the friends, family, teachers, pastors, professors, and guides who have believed in me over the years. Your support has meant the world to me. I would specifically like to thank Joya for helping me with my creativity and articulation through the writing process.

I would also like to thank the many students I have served in ministry. I have learned a lot from each of you. You are wonderful blessings.

Of course, I would also like to thank God. Without the love of Christ, none of this would be possible.

Introduction

THE SEA OF LIFE is vast and ever-changing. Our time on the shore is brief, so a time comes for all wherein we must face the grand expanse. Some pilot their vessels alone through the waters, while others board metaphorical ocean liners, filled to the brim with travelers. Many ships have the express purpose of helping those who have become overwhelmed by the waves. Some of those ships bear the flag of Christian ministry. Of all the kinds of boats upon life's ocean, I am particularly familiar with those. A few years ago, in fact, I jumped onto the side of a ministry ship, and it has since left port. However, I am unable to climb aboard. I write this, then, from my precarious perch on the side of the ministry ship. Far removed from shore by now, and yet still not quite a crewman, I try to make the most of my situation.

What I mean to say, through figurative language, is that I am presently in an interesting place. I find myself in-between the worlds of clergy and laity, with all the joys and difficulties that such a status brings. Today, I am a servant in youth ministry. Educated, though not yet decorated, committed entirely to ministry, yet not officially ordained, my role exists in something akin to a state of limbo. In many respects, it has always been that way.

In the contemporary church, I have never been an insider. However, despite my ostensible presence in the outsider camp, I am not exactly an outcast, either. In my elementary, middle, and high school days, I was never exactly popular, or overly articulate, or otherwise impressive in such a way as to be included within the

Introduction

lauded "in-crowd." However, I had knowledge and my disposition was pleasant, and I interacted with others enough, so that I did maintain some standing in the social realm and in church circles.

Today, I am a student in ministry school, in addition to my volunteer service in youth ministry. Despite such a role in the church, I am not quite on the inside of the ministry world. Since I am currently unpaid for my ministry efforts, the countless hours I invest in ministry and the extensive amount of exhaustive effort I pour forth does little to validate my calling in the eyes of some people.

Make no mistake, ministry consumes me. I help plan events, I teach, I preach, and I perform baptisms. However, regardless of my passion, my lack of a paycheck or pastoral title is enough for many to view me as an outsider in the world of ministry. I knock on the doors of affirmation, but typically find them locked from within.

This book is my way of showcasing my perspective and insights. My voice has always been on the periphery, but through my writing here, I am able to have a central platform, from which to share my views, for the first time in my life. I write this as a 22-year-old ministry student and ministry servant. My intention is to speak largely on behalf of young people, including the ones I serve today. I am not far removed from teenage years myself, and that recency, combined with my present status, lends a duality to my perspective, which informs the beliefs I now put forth.

My ultimate hope is that it is God who speaks through me on these pages. After all, I am far from perfect. I sin, I slip, I fall, and I am only human. Therefore, it is best if the notions I put forth, in this writing, are not my own but instead come from God. In truth, I can do nothing of my own power. My wish is that I may tap into wisdom and truth which exist beyond me, so that notions that are from God may be transmitted on these pages. I hope to follow in the footsteps of many authors before me, whose conveyances of such ambrosial truth inspire me to share likewise.

In the coming pages, I will be sharing a number of insights that I have gathered over the years, both from my time as a young

INTRODUCTION

member of various youth ministries and as a servant of youth in my current ministry role. I will begin each chapter with a section dedicated to articulating my thoughts about the subject at hand. After that, I will share personal experiences that may shed light upon how my beliefs regarding these various matters came to be. Lastly, I have closed each section with a question, so that the discussion may not end where my words do.

Thank you for taking the time to read what lies ahead, and may God guide us all ever-forward in the way of Jesus.

1

When the "Bad Kids" Get Marginalized

MY THOUGHTS

In nearly every gathering of youth, at least one student is singled out in some spoken or unspoken way as the "bad kid." Sometimes, multiple students get this undesirable reputation. The reaction toward these characters is generally the same. After a few attempts at some manner of initial outreach, slowly but surely people withdraw, leaving the rejected young person on the margins. I have been guilty of marginalizing so-called "bad kids" in this way. In my younger days, I suffered some exclusion myself.

The key to resolving this painful group dynamic is to dissolve the stereotype of the "bad kid" among our youth. The very notion of a "bad kid" has some similarities to the old idiom of the "black sheep" in a family or among friends. In both cases, an outsider to a group is regarded as an aberration of an unstated norm—someone who deserves to be shunned and sidelined. The sheep metaphor instantly reminds me of how God is sometimes described through shepherd imagery. Like a shepherd who leaves the ninety-nine sheep behind in order to find the one who has gone astray, so God actively seeks out the "black sheep" and the "bad kid" (Matthew

18:12–14). God does the exact opposite of what we in the church often do. Shouldn't we imitate God? We should welcome the outcast. Let us, with love, search for the "bad kids," as God searches for the missing sheep.

In ministry and as Christians, it is advisable to behave in a Christlike manner toward everyone, certainly toward all the youth, and especially toward those whom some may consider "bad kids." The so-called "bad" people are just like us. Is a boat with fifty small holes in it any more seaworthy than a boat with a massive break in its hull? No. Even if we may presume that we have fewer "holes" in our character than the so-called "bad people," whom some are tempted to see as massively broken, in truth we are all faulty vessels in relation to God. We are all dependent on the love of Christ to keep us afloat. It is Jesus Christ's calm presence on the boat, as we may recall, which calms our fears and the storms of life (Mark 4:35–41). Even if we don't consciously hold a view of ourselves as superior to others, or actively boast that we have fewer flaws than those other broken boats (i.e., the "bad kids"), such arrogance can still creep into our subconscious and influence our actions. We must examine our hearts, and try to remove our biases.

Far from simply making an internal evaluation and pondering through our best intentions, this practice of compassion toward the "bad kids" should translate into decisive action. By extending a Christlike helping hand to those who are struggling (with any number of difficulties), we can help to break down the walls that separate the so-called "good" and "bad" kids.

The compassion of Jesus toward outsiders is our greatest example. Jesus was known for causing scandal by associating with the "wrong" people. The upper echelons of society so looked down upon the "sinners" (e.g., prostitutes, juvenile delinquents, thieves, and other misfits) that they were appalled that Jesus would not only associate himself but actually have dinner with this "bad" group (Mark 2:16). When was the last time we associated with people who had such a reputation for being outcasts that in-crowd people were all aghast to find us in their presence? When was the last time we were known for going out of our way to associate with the "bad kids"?

If, as a minister, or just as a believer, you are unafraid to associate with this kind of youth, then you are on the right path. Unfortunately, not all of us make a habit of this behavior, even though it is clearly the Christlike option. Social pressure is a powerful dissuader. Nonetheless, we must look to the example of Christ, so that social pressure never usurps the will of God. If the so-called "insiders" turn on us because of our love for the outsiders, then so be it. We may rest assured that we are loving as Jesus loves. Let us remain undaunted by any dangers or penalties for such compassion.

Our love for others must never be contingent on selfish motives—like what we can gain from showing love or how the love may benefit us personally. If we are wanting social standing and recognition from love, then we are misguided in the first place. If our love is an outpouring of the love that Christ has poured into us, however, then this love will identify us as people of faith. We place faith in a greater power of love, to which the passing fancies of this present world (such as social recognition) cannot be compared.

The "bad kids" often get left out of our ministries. We see them as too odd, too coarse, or too dangerous. This is a horribly misguided way to look at things. We must replace the limited vision of our human perception with the unlimited vision of Jesus. We must replace our biases, fears, and hatred with the pure love of Christ. So many wander around like the one sheep that left the ninety-nine. The love of Christ shepherds them even in their wandering. Christ is present with them already, and thus, since we are Christians, we should follow Christ. We should be with the outcasts, as that is where Christ can be found.

The "bad kids" among our youth deserve our care. We should be willing to seek them out with Christlike love. We should never let them become ostracized because of our own fear for our reputations. We are all flawed, in our own ways. Christ's love overcomes these flaws, for each of us. Therefore, we should never act superior to the youth who get labelled as "bad." Instead, we must always extend Christlike compassion to the outcasts in our churches and communities.

MY EXPERIENCE

My Youth Experience

In my middle school years, there was a group of students at the church I attended who were known for their rough exterior. These were the kids from the proverbial wrong side of the tracks. These kids acted out, created issues, spoke coarsely, and engaged in questionable activities. For many of their church leaders, these factors were dealbreakers. Instead of reaching out to those students, the leaders washed their hands of them. The students were tolerated, rather than ministered to.

The kids I knew personally from among that group were actually wonderful people. They were not perfect, of course, but neither am I. (In truth, who is, except God?) Beneath their tough exteriors, they were people who knew compassion, loyalty, and love. The "rough" students were far from being the band of brigands that they were often painted as being. They were just as caring and empathetic as many within the in-crowd group at that church. Many of the outsiders were perhaps even more compassionate than their revered peers.

Unfortunately, most of the leaders in that church were never able to see these students for who they truly were. This reality caused me to feel dejected, for I knew the truth that I was no better than those "outcasts." If they were objects of such shunning, what made me deserve any better? What made anyone deserve any better?

My Servant Experience

Recently, I attended a large gathering of several youth groups. Many interesting people attended, from a variety of different backgrounds. I came to this gathering with a group of students, but while there I made new connections as well.

I met one group of students, in particular, from another church a few states away. Before very long, we became friends. I spent a lot of time with them during the week. These fast friends of mine were outsiders, in their own way. Though rather crude and offensive to some, these youth did not repel me. I saw through their rough exteriors. How they were acting, that week, did not truly represent who they were. In my many conversations with them, I learned that they were actually a very nice bunch of fellows. One even wanted to be a pastor. Another told me about how tough things were in the city they were from and how they would be kept up some nights by the sound of gunshots. This was an experience not shared by many at that conference.

Many at that conference looked down upon this group, regarding them as outcasts. I was reminded throughout that week of how Jesus never feared to associate with so-called outcasts. I enjoyed my time with the group. My experience taught me the importance of giving everyone a chance. When a person does so, great treasures may be uncovered. God's kingdom belongs to the outcasts.

CLOSING QUESTION

What can we do to break down the systems in our midst that tend to create in-crowds and out-crowds?

2

The Union of Optimism and Honesty

MY THOUGHTS

THE WORLD CAN BE a difficult place. Most everyone feels downtrodden at times, and youth are no exception. Many things can bring a person down, from the political climate and wars, to issues at home and in relationships. These burdens can be crushing to a young person's happiness. However, Christ offers us hope in the midst of all our struggles. This hope can be championed in our youth ministries.

Holding onto hope and a positive outlook is not easy for everyone to sustain. We are all human beings, after all, and troubles can easily make their way to our doors. Some would propose that we hide our struggles from the youth, so that younger people will not be discouraged by the difficulties of their older siblings in the faith. This reasoning is understandable, since we would not want the faith of our youth to waver because they witness our dire straits. If we make a policy of never showing our struggles, however, and if we choose to portray ourselves as people who are never troubled by life's difficulties, then we may create untrustworthy images of ourselves. Our false image of constant tranquility could

The Union of Optimism and Honesty

be catastrophic to the faith that young people place in us. Thus, I do not advocate committing to an optimism about life that is not grounded in the reality of struggle. We can, and do face struggles in this world—and these struggles will persist through life.

Some would suggest an opposite strategy for youth ministries. This approach would have us repeatedly and unendingly focus on our struggles. In this vein, we could use our unfiltered difficulties to showcase how the world is a challenging place. Youth will then not be surprised when they encounter such difficulties as well. This method of reasoning is understandable to some degree, as it counters the "fake Christian" stereotype, where a believer pretends to have nothing but happiness in life, with no problems. This method of reasoning, however, goes to the other extreme. As a remedy for the difficulties of the world that it so readily acknowledges, this approach may point young believers away from this world entirely, and towards God's perfect world, which is far greater than the one we currently find ourselves in. While there is certainly some truth to the idea that God's perfect realm far surpasses our own, this perspective could lead to an unhealthy worldview. Despite its faults, our current world has been created by God, and goodness still exists here. A steady diet of pessimism about our current home could cause a variety of spiritual ills. According to this perspective, we may be permitted to be filled with a loathing toward the world. However, God certainly does not intend for believers to hold that sort of pessimism and hatred for the world in our hearts.

My approach to youth ministry, in this regard, is a middle ground, between the two extremes. In one sense, I do believe that there is a definite place for optimism in our worldview. It is worthwhile to project our lives in a positive light. We do have a tremendous hope in Christ, and this hope should always inform our actions and disposition. At the same time, as Scripture makes clear, there is a certain beauty in lamenting the struggles and difficulties in the world. Books like Ecclesiastes, Jeremiah, and Lamentations (naturally), among others, bear out this point. To be honest about the difficulties that we face, and even to cry out to God in such times is far from "sinful." In fact, these laments are a good and healthy part of our relationship with God. Just as honesty about our struggles can build trust with the youth, so likewise it can help our relationship with God. Christ already knows our hearts, but we should still feel free to bare them. In doing so, we lead by example. Our youth will learn that it is natural to be honest and open about our feelings, even the difficult ones. Therefore, honesty about our difficulties may be combined with optimism. Whatever our plight, we ultimately find our hope in Christ Jesus.

In summary, we should represent our own lives honestly but with a hopeful and optimistic faith in God. How then shall we speak into the lives of youth? When young people face struggles, they have no doubt already learned that the world can be a difficult place. Thus, it is imperative to speak positivity into their situation. In particular, we should always point them primarily to God's love and to the hope we have in Christ, despite the trials and tribulations that we face.

In doing so, we will allow them to recognize God's constant love, despite all that they may be going through. God still loves them. Nothing can separate us from God's love in Christ (Romans 8:38–39). By meditating on this truth, one discovers the key to facing our difficulties in the world. God's amazing care for us all provides endless hope and encouragement. Because of this, the youth may be encouraged to reside and abide in the love of Christ.

By pointing them toward the hope we have in Christ, we provide an important grounding for their faith in a tangible reality that awaits us. Once joined to this hope, we may follow in the footsteps of Abraham, who also awaited God's eternal city (Hebrews 11:10). This wonderful hope should never be confused with an easy escapism. Instead, hope should bolster our collective faith in the present and inspire us all to live out God's calling, as citizens of the great city of the age to come. When our youth are brought this glorious vision, the troubles of our world are no longer worth comparing to what is to come (Romans 8:18). Problems are not altogether erased, nor do pains magically disappear. However, difficulties become more bearable when put into perspective; our troubles now are just a phase in God's cosmic redemptive work.

Our youth struggle, just as we do. We should never hide the fact that we, too, struggle. However, we should always brighten honest descriptions of our struggles with the truth of God's love and the hope we have in Christ Jesus. In doing so, we show young people that tough times will come, but that God has given us the strength to endure.

MY EXPERIENCE

My Youth Experience

I remember an instance where a church leader showing only optimism led to quite a interesting situation. During my middle school years, I had one particular teacher in church who was known for positivity without realism. He would often tout the upside of Christianity, but rarely if ever would he point out how struggles are still faced by Christians, just as they are faced by everyone.

One time, after one of this teacher's messages, a rather "unchurched" friend remarked to me how fake it all seemed. The friend snidely remarked that the teacher probably took out his whiskey flask when we all had our heads bowed in prayer. The implication there was that the teacher acted as though life had no difficulties while he had our attention, yet he secretly struggled with alcoholism. While my friend's comment itself was foolish and baseless on a number of levels, I think his satirical humor struck at something noteworthy. The teacher's positivity lacked balance, reinforcing the "fake Christian" stereotype in the minds of some students.

From that point onward, I paid close attention to different teachers, to see which ones spoke about difficulties and which ones did not. While I have no doubt that the positivity-only teachers meant well, and I respect them for their teaching efforts (especially now, since I am often the one in the teacher's shoes), I keep a special place in my heart for teachers who are not afraid to discuss struggles and difficulties.

My Servant Experience

At the church I currently attend, there are a lot of hallways. In those hallways, an interesting phenomenon occurs. During a busy Sunday, people frequently pass by each other, and when they do, they often ask each other how they are doing. The canned response that instantly fires back, in almost all instances, is a simple "Fine, how are you?"

Every now and then, however, that default response will be met with a follow-up question: "No, really, how are you doing?" While this kind of question is uncommon, it does happen on occasion, and when it does, it can be a real shock to the system. I say this as someone who has been on the receiving end of that follow-up question a time or two.

This phenomenon speaks to something important within the church as a whole. Often times, we feel the need to put up a facade of optimism, even when we are struggling. When someone breaks through that facade, it can lead to some very helpful and important conversations. I have tried to invite such conversations in my youth ministry service. Teenagers, just like their adult counterparts, have been trained by society's unwritten rules to respond to the question of "How are you?" with a basic answer of positivity. However, there are times when they are far from "doing well," and they desperately need someone to talk to. At those times, it is vitally important to allow conversations to take place. Those genuine exchanges can only be had if the initial facade of unmitigated optimism is broken. From there, honesty springs forth.

CLOSING QUESTION

If our optimism and honesty are at odds, how can we go about fusing the two together so that our optimism is honest, and our honesty is not without optimism?

3

Striving to be Peacemakers

MY THOUGHTS

CHRIST PROCLAIMS A BLESSING to peacemakers (Matthew 5:9). The role of peacemaker is often overlooked in our world of conflict, division, and war. Movies star fighters, warriors, and killers. Many popular video games today glorify killing and violence. Combat and conflict are parts of our society, whether we like that reality or not. Violence is glamorized, combat is commercialized, and war is marketed. In a land of such aggressive tendencies, it isn't always easy to live out God's call to be peacemakers, in any context. Despite the challenges, peacemaking is certainly a path of righteousness, since we serve the Prince of Peace (Isaiah 9:6).

In the context of youth ministry, conflict is just as prevalent as it can be among older people. The reasons for conflict can range from trivial to serious. No matter the reason, our role as followers of Christ should always be to seek out peace in situations of conflict.

The role of peacemaker can draw ire from all the parties involved in a conflict. Nonetheless, the witness of peacemakers, who pour themselves out in love, for the purpose of peace, is impactful and very difficult to ignore. When we stick to living out Christ's love, people will take notice. Eventually, our peacemaking may persuade those involved in the conflict to put aside their differences for the sake of love and unity. Even if we are unsuccessful, we should not be discouraged. Our faithfulness to Christ should not falter, even when victory is prolonged.

Even if the overwhelming quality of our compassion and love in the midst of conflict may strike combatants as odd, we must take heart that we are fulfilling our roles as ministers of reconciliation (2 Corinthians 5:11–21). We should not hesitate to show love to all people, including youth when they find themselves embroiled in conflict with one another. Even Peter and Paul found themselves at odds at least once (Galatians 2:11–14). Just as Christ no doubt still loved both of those apostles in that moment of strife, we should continue to love those locked in conflict. Perhaps our love will warm their hearts and melt their icy feuds. Who can say? What we must do is remain faithful to God's call to peacemaking.

A common type of conflict that I've witnessed, both as a youth and while serving in youth ministry, is fueled by an athletic rivalry between two or more youngsters (who may be especially competitive). Such rivalries are by no means trivial, for they can get quite vicious. How, then, can we pour Christ's love into such a situation? Initially, we can try to diffuse the tension by affirming the skill set of all the competitors. We thus equalize the playing field while simultaneously diffusing the intensity of the competition. After the initial wave of tensions has subsided, we may proceed to question the very nature of the competition, as such contests can bring out qualities in people that are not very Christlike. The example of Christ is always our guide. Would Christ take part in a competition that gets so heated, that it drives a wedge between believers? I am inclined to think not. Therefore, we should encourage a Christlike peacemaking approach, particularly for those with maturity enough to handle and accept such a path.

To diffuse conflict can take many forms. The key is to pour Christlike love into conflictual situations. We should be willing to sacrifice our own well being, and our own interests, for the sake of maintaining unity, peace, and love. To represent Christ by pointing people toward God's love should be of the utmost importance. The love of Christ, which diffuses conflict, does not always make its efficacy obvious. Consider the moment Christ was being crucified. This sacrifice dispelled the conflict between humankind and the dark forces of this world. Through it, Jesus was drawing all people to himself (John 12:32). From the outside, the crucifixion may have appeared like a loss and a hopeless defeat. In times of defeat and loss, we must remember that God is still working behind the scenes, and therefore it is imperative that we cling not to ourselves, but to Christ. In doing so, our peacemaking will not be in vain.

MY EXPERIENCE

My Youth Experience

In high school, I spent some time in a youth ministry that had quite sharp divisions within it. The group was around a 50–50 split between students who were in the "in-crowd," of the churchgoing variety, and students who were rougher around the edges and outside of the churchgoing mold. I was friends with people on both sides of this divide, which made me one of the few students who could get along with both camps. For the most part, the two sides did not associate with one another.

The factional differences came to a head, eventually, and threatened to split the ministry. Tensions were high, with each side feeling as though the other side was out to get them. Neither side had very kind words for the other. As someone in the middle, who struggled to maintain my place on the fence, I began to attract animosity. Both groups were not particularly fond of how I (and a few others) maintained friendships with their rivals. It was a very sad state of affairs, and many ended up drifting away from the ministry as a result.

In the end, most of the central figures on the two sides went away, but not before leaving behind deep scars in the ministry. One of the starkest images of the divisions occurred during group gatherings. A large gap of empty seats between the two sides would open up, like a canyon between two imposing mountains. There was no peace there, and it was a sad thing to behold.

My Servant Experience

These days, my summers typically involve volunteering for a week of youth camp. Some great memories are made, but these times are not without their occasional difficulties. In such a relatively isolated environment for a week, the competitive spirit runs high, leading to some conflicts from time to time.

One recent summer, in particular, there were two rival cabins, which each held groups formed from two different regions, one from due east of where the camp is located and one from the west. The competition between these two sides got intense, at times, as each side sought to represent where they came from to the best of their ability. The aggressive competition between the two sides hurt the chemistry of the camp as a whole.

While the tensions between the two sides eventually cooled, that experience highlights how quickly peace can be eroded within youth ministry. As someone who serves youth, I have to remain on my toes in order to promote peace and cohesion between factions. In a perfect world, there would be no such factions at all. Until that is the case, however, we must be peacemakers, promoting unity, empathy, and compassion in all circumstances.

CLOSING QUESTION

What are some ways in which we can work to prevent conflict before it occurs?

4

Encouraging Curiosity

MY THOUGHTS

Curiosity is a wonderful thing. Often times, however, curiosity or inquisitiveness can be seen as intimidating, particularly when expressed by young people. A common worry concerns our uncertainty, should we lack answers to the questions they raise. It is understandable that one might fear causing discouragement, and potentially causing someone's faith to waver, if we lack sufficient answers. The benefits of curiosity, however, far exceed any potential risks.

The quest for knowledge and answers can lead toward a more developed relationship with God. Jesus reminds us that our seeking leads to finding (Matthew 7:7–8). Upon further investigation, we may ask ourselves how one could possibly find something if they weren't seeking that thing. Further, to seek something means that one is curious to some degree. Because of this connection, it seems as though curiosity is integral to a healthy process of spiritual growth.

Curiosity helps to unravel mysteries. Paul gladly proclaims the mysterious things of God (1 Corinthians 2:6–7). His preaching no doubt met with curiosity on the part of many. They proclaimed

Christ to be Lord as a result. Curious people seek answers. This quest for understanding can lead a person toward further study, further meditation, and further thought. These pursuits can be incredibly beneficial for enhancing one's relationship with God. The more we know about God, the more we know of Christ's love. Because of the boundlessness of such love, which can never be grasped fully, there will always be greater depths for us to discover. Curiosity is a great fuel for the quest.

One of the greatest things we can do for the youth is to serve as guides as they walk their paths of curiosity. Many of us have been through the same internal questioning and quests for truth that many young people find themselves on today. God can use our own experiences; let's be willing to share them in order to help guide and encourage the young folks around us.

Our own walk during our youth can be very important to our dynamic with the younger people of the present. If we were very curious, it is likely we will be able to relate to youngsters who are equally curious today. This shared curiosity could even go a long way toward breaking down the divide that sometimes exists between younger and older believers. Sometimes our role isn't that of guide but rather that of travel partner. If we are stumped by questions and their curiosity, we may still walk alongside them on their journey, so that we, too, may make our way to a deeper understanding.

While growing up, I would often find myself questioning one theological belief or another. Rarely did anyone come alongside of me, whether as a guide or a companion on the journey. I cannot emphasize enough how difficult it was to search for my way alone, in an attempt to satiate my curiosity. Thankfully, God was very merciful to me, and my curiosity led me closer to Christ in the long run. Nonetheless, my difficulties would have been relieved, or at least made much easier to endure, if someone had been there for me as a guide or companion.

Therefore, let us keep a keen eye out for signs of curiosity in our youth. A young person may always seem to be listening intently during theological discussions or they may always be asking questions. I was often the one with the questions. I still find myself asking a ton of questions. For some people, their nature is to be inquisitive, which can be beneficial to their relationship with God. Let's rejoice when youth are on a journey of curiosity, and do all that we can to assist them.

Curiosity is a wonderful gift. When we recognize and celebrate curiosity, we dispel the stigma that can exist around inquisitiveness in the church. In a misguided attempt to preserve the faith of others, some try to stifle curiosity. Curiosity is a blessing; searching for answers often leads to finding those answers and more. Opening one's mind through inquisitiveness develops a respect for truth and compassion for different perspectives. Curiosity can bring a person into a deeper and more vibrant relationship with God and other people. That is a blessed thing, indeed.

MY EXPERIENCE

My Youth Experience

In some of the more fundamentalist church circles in which I grew up, curiosity was hardly seen as a positive thing. Questions were often discouraged. At the very least, the toughest questions were avoided. As someone who is known for his inquisitiveness, and has been since a very early age (I won the "Most Inquisitive" award in my third grade class), a shutdown of open questioning was disheartening.

Being the kid who always asked "Why?" did not exactly endear me to some of my instructors. Repeated questioning was seen as a lack of faith. However, I was (and still am) of the opinion that faith does not have to be uninformed in order to be pleasing to God. Questions can bring many a person closer to God.

I believe that the more we truly learn about God, the more we learn to love God. This has certainly been the case for me. Even when we think our knowledge and love of God are at their peak, they manage to grow even greater still. Curiosity and questions are often a vital part of this process, so to stifle such things can get in the way of spiritual growth. Thankfully, my penchant for questions was not extinguished in my younger days, and it is still going strong.

My Servant Experience

While teaching the high schoolers that I serve today, I often find that there are some among them who are very curious and inquisitive individuals. This always brings me joy, as I see curiosity as an avenue toward a greater relationship with God. I am always eager to receive questions, and to respond to them to the best of my understanding.

One time recently, I was giving a lesson to the students about the afterlife. I was discussing things such as heaven, hell, and so on. At the end of the talk, I was sure to mention that, if anyone had questions that they didn't want to air out for everyone to hear, they could talk to me in private about those things. Both in my younger days and in the present, questions about heaven, hell, and the like tend to be the most maligned and scrutinized by the anti-curiosity types, so I knew that some might have had questions that they would rather ask in private, away from prying ears.

One student did, in fact, reach out to me after that lesson. He and I discussed how his view of hell was somewhere in the universalist camp. This position is one I am open to discussing, but it is certainly not a popular opinion with many in churches today, so I definitely understood why this particular student wanted to discuss his views in a private setting. He and I ended up having a very nice and thought-provoking discussion about hell, and this may never have happened if I had not gone out of my way to encourage questions and curiosity. A curious mind is fertile ground, so we must nurture it as such.

CLOSING QUESTION

What can we do to encourage more curiosity from youth in our churches?

5

Eccentricities are Blessings

MY THOUGHTS

Picture a vast field of freshly tilled soil. What do you expect of this field? I currently live near fields where corn and soy are the usual suspects. Countless seedlings can be identified in our fields as they take their first glances at the blue sky above. However, every passing witness may picture the new plants differently as they emerge from earthen homes. What you picture the field becoming may be based on your preferences and expectations. Whatever you picture, there is some reason for your choice. Something has led to your expectations for our hypothetical field.

As you may be able to guess, our imaginary field represents something very real. Our youth are the field. More specifically, our youth are the seedlings within the field. In fact, the kingdom of God itself grows like a field, even though we cannot comprehend the true depth to such a mystery (Mark 4:26–29). Unlike the plants in the fields that we picture, our youth are not all destined to grow into a single, uniform crop. Their destinies are not all the same. Nonetheless, we often try to force them to conform to a certain standard that is suitable only for a few people. We want young people to become "something" (a "something" that confirms to our own value system). So, we shape them accordingly, even if, in doing so, we are tearing away crucial parts of their nature and personality.

Now, there is an important point that I must clarify here. I do not mean that we should stop shaping our youth (and ourselves) according to the mold given to us by Christ. We ought all to follow Christ's example, embodying Christlike love and radical sacrifice. Our ultimate goal is the imitation of Christ (1 Corinthians 11:1), which deepens our communion with God. Therefore, I am warning against shaping our youth into a mold that is not from God, since such shaping can draw them far away from the one model for us all to follow: Jesus Christ.

The erroneous mold that we often force upon our youth is formed by human standards and expectations. For example, we often want our youth to be successful, according to society's standards of success. Such standards and expectations inevitably lead our youth down a dangerous path, making it ultimately more difficult for them to achieve an authentic transformation into disciples (which God calls them to be).

Let us consider an example, to illustrate the negative outcomes of such coercion. Let's say a student behaves in an eccentric manner. Their youth leaders and peers are troubled by such stark nonconformity. Through pointed leadership coupled with peer pressure, they mold this youngster in such a way that the student sheds his or her former eccentricities. The formerly eccentric student becomes like the rest of the group in terms of manner, interests, and demeanor. However, in this process, the student loses all of the treasures of individuality that were hidden in the eccentricity. No longer can this student relate to others who share his or her bygone eccentric ways. No longer do someone's unique traits serve in unique places and ways. If Student A loves unicycling, for instance, but Student A's leaders and peers ban unicycling as if this recreation were too eccentric an activity for a "good" Christian, then student A may abandon a passion for unicycling. This person will no longer be glorifying God through unicycling. The community has lost the richness of someone's passion and talent.

What, then, is the alternative to molding our youth in misguided ways? As previously indicated, youth do not grow with such uniformity as one expects from a corn or wheat field. Instead of pushing them toward such uniformity, we should affirm the unique nuances of the individual's nature and personality. Each person can glorify God and follow Christ in their own unique way. We should praise God for this and not try to work against God's manner of operating through this process of growth. Let us not be eager to stamp out quirks. Instead, quirks and idiosyncrasies can be potential blessings, which God has bestowed upon each of us so that we may reflect Christ's love in unique ways and contexts. These blessings should certainly be praised, and neither feared nor fought against.

We are enriched by embracing the uniqueness of our youth. I was unique as a youngster, myself, (and I still am). I can speak from my own experience. I grew and flourished, and truly felt like a part of God's family, when people accepted me for who I am, eccentricities and all. When forced into a mold that did not fit, I felt as though I were not good enough to be in God's family. I'm sure many others have similar experiences. Christ's teachings show us that God's family is inclusive. This inclusive reality can be exhibited by our ways of treating all the different varieties of unique personalities among our youth. Instead of treating the eccentrics as outsiders, we should welcome their blessings among us.

MY EXPERIENCE

My Youth Experience

As I mentioned, I was often the eccentric kid growing up. I had eclectic interests, which were not shared by the majority of people I knew. While I was often in church as a youngster, I did not find much respite there. My eccentricity or "weirdness" was sometimes tolerated, but other times, not so much.

In my younger years, I was often bullied for being that kid who was really fascinated by science and history, while most other boys my age were only interested in sports. While the bullying upset me, it thankfully did not dissuade me from being interested in a wide variety of subjects of learning.

The theological side of my fascinations did not come until a bit later, although my interest in learning showed itself in church as well. Particularly in middle school, I would be entranced by facets of Bible stories, particularly in the Old Testament. For instance, I would ask why Balaam did not appear to be all that surprised that his donkey spoke to him (Numbers 22:21–39). While most of my peers were excited to just be done with Bible reading, I would be stuck on questions like that which popped up as I went through the text.

As I moved on into high school, I was still the eccentric student. At that point, my interests were even wider and more eclectic than they had been before. At one moment, I could be speaking passionately about the symbolism of heavy metal music, and the next moment could find me spouting a philosophical theory regarding time. My peers at the church I attended, at this point, were less than subtle about their annoyance with me. It was around this time that it became clear to me that I was indeed a different sort of Christian. While my unique interests were not enough to make me a complete outsider, there were certainly enough curiosities to bar me from ever entering into the hallowed "in-crowd." This was a source of great dejection for me, and it eventually prompted me to take an extended period of time away from church. Thankfully, God did not abandon me, even when my peers did.

My Servant Experience

Because of my past experiences, I am now keen as a server of youth to look out for those who may be eccentrics in their own right. I know that they have valuable gifts to contribute to the church as a whole, but so often they slip between the cracks when their peers avoid them because they do not understand them. I always try to extend a helping hand to the eccentric students, so that they know I intend to be supportive of them.

Just as things were in my younger days, students who march to the beat of a different drum are often maligned today. I have learned that this is something that ministry servants should always be mindful of. These students are treasures to Christ, but their ostracization at the hands of their peers can often make them feel worthless. We should never allow Christ's treasures to feel worthless.

As with other issues, I cannot help but wonder what system within the church as a whole leads to ostracizing some youth because they do not conform to certain norms. It seems obvious to me from a plain reading of Scripture that the church is to be a diverse unit, so it stands to reason that differences in personality and interests should be praised, not castigated. Blessed are the unique. Blessed are the eccentrics.

CLOSING QUESTION

What are some ways within the church in which we can highlight the unique gifts that each person has been given by God?

6

Compassionate Actions

MY THOUGHTS

Compassion serves as a hallmark of the Christian faith. To pour love into every situation may sound like an obvious imperative, but in the hustle and bustle of life, this imperative often gets ignored. We pass by people, each and every day, who feel lost and dejected. They are in need of love and support. However, not only do people typically not notice their pain, but sometimes, any lamentation of it is discouraged. The same is true among our youth. Often times, young folks are going through suffering and sorrow that we cannot even imagine.

In my time as a youth volunteer, I have gained insight from the struggles faced by young people. Many times I have been surprised and caught off guard by the sufferings and difficulties shared by a youngster. Very real and complex issues confront our youth. We should never belittle or trivialize their issues. They need compassion, just like the rest of us.

Compassion should inform our mindset and interactions. If we are distracted, we may not notice what is right in front of us. Sometimes, a simple conversation moves us toward compassion. It is beneficial to foster an environment of openness and transparency in youth ministry. If the youth know it is perfectly acceptable, and even encouraged, to share their struggles in an honest and unfiltered way, then they will also be more inclined to do so.

Imagine for a moment that you were seeking buried treasure. You must go on quite a long journey to find the treasure in question. You face many obstacles along the way, but nothing that arises can shake your resolve, because the thought of the treasure remains ever at the forefront of your mind. Similarly, compassion should be at the forefront of our minds. No matter what we face, or the hurdles we must jump through, no difficulty will be able to bring us down if compassion is our priority. As long as we stay centered in Christlike compassion for others, we will be on the right path.

Our goal should be to bring our youth toward a lifestyle that is driven by compassion. Society can be vicious and unforgiving, and this is no different for youth. A drive to be the best, the most popular, or the most successful is a force that compels all of us, sometimes with devastating consequences. To fully embrace compassion, one must (to some extent) let go of such drives. We should encourage our youth to place compassion before acquisition.

As ambassadors for Christ, we must not fall victim to the traps set for us by the dark forces of this present world. If we set a good example in this, the youth are sure to take notice. Instead of finding themselves locked in a sort of Darwinian struggle with their peers, our youth could be pouring out love to those around them, at all times. In doing so, a great many lives could be changed for the better.

We should embody compassion, both so that we may follow Christ and so that our youth may follow our example. The world is starved of love. So often, we fail to show the world the compassion that it so desperately needs. We should pray that God may open our senses to the needs around us so that we may pour out love in response. May we always show compassion to our youth, and may they come to embody compassion as well.

MY EXPERIENCE

My Youth Experience

Growing up, I was not nearly as altruistic as I would like to say I was. I was often near the bottom of the social pecking order, but instead of accepting that position with grace and humility, I often found myself fighting against it. In doing so, I sometimes forgot about the others like me, who were also struggling near the bottom of the food chain. I let detached pragmatism override my love of neighbor.

In order to cover my insecurities, I would typically try to join the in-group, both at school and in youth ministry. This never went all that well, and generally led to disappointment, but I kept at it. I was so concerned with protecting myself by moving up the social ladder, that I lost track of those who were struggling along with me.

This was, in some respects, a dark time in my life. I had let my compassion become compromised by the cares of this world. That is always a bad situation to be in. While I did eventually grow out of that phase, I am hit hard when I think of all the good that I could have done in those days, but that I failed to do. If only I had allowed compassion to take center stage, instead of my own fragile ego, I can only dream of what positive things could have been accomplished. There were no doubt many people I could have been there for along the way, instead of just looking out for myself.

My Servant Experience

Though I have learned over the years the importance of compassion, I still slip away from it on occasion. There are still times in which I let my emotions get the best of me. Instead of stopping to let empathy and compassion take hold of my heart, I sometimes dive into a situation before I have even had a chance to think about what the most Christlike response may be.

One such event was at a youth retreat where I served several months ago. There, tensions among students would quickly flare up on occasion. At one point, things got so intense between two students, that they became very close to a physical altercation. Instead of acting like a Christlike mediator, I let my emotions get the best of me and I reacted with anger. I ended up using some harsh words toward one of the involved students. I am not proud of such a moment, but it serves as a reminder to me that learning to embody compassion is a long journey. Unfortunately, there will be issues along the way.

As someone who tends to pride himself on having a calm temperament, that incident took a toll on me. After it, though, I have recommitted myself to striving to emulate Christ in every situation. When the compassion of Christ shines through, tensions will often resolve for the best. We cannot allow our emotions to override Christ's calling. I learned that the hard way.

CLOSING QUESTION

What are some ways in which we can maintain a heart of compassion, even in the most trying of circumstances?

7

The Voices of Our Youth

MY THOUGHTS

EVERY PERSON HAS A unique perspective to bring to the table. These perspectives can mesh together beautifully to strengthen the diverse unity of the Church. Our youth have a unique voice as well, although they are sadly ignored quite often by many adults. This is a shame, as youth have very important insights to contribute to our collective conversation as believers.

Every generation is different. Because of that, every generation has its own collective experience, different from those of previous generations. With this collective experience comes certain traits, from mannerisms and sayings, to worldviews and moral stances. Our youth have their set of generational traits, and these can prove quite helpful to the growth and development of believers as a whole.

For example, many youth today are passionate about social and civil reform. In fact, they could probably lead a lot of the adults in the church with regard to these issues. Their passion for reform and justice can spread to other generations, if given the proper platform. This is a wonderful thing, as it shows how each generation has something unique to contribute to the other generations in a church. We can each help one another, as a collective unit. Christ can speak through anyone, no matter what others may think of them. Humankind cannot dictate to God exactly who God will choose as an instrument or vessel to move through. God's mercy determines how such things will come to pass, not human desire or machinations (Romans 9:16).

Sometimes people marginalize the voices of youth because they simply haven't "lived enough" yet, as though life experience were the only path to spiritual understanding. Let's not forget that Jesus chided the disciples for keeping the children away from Him (Matthew 19:13–15). Let us also not hold to such hubris that we believe we are in some way superior to those who are younger than us. We each have something to teach one another, and we each have something to learn from one another. When we accept this reality with openness, we can learn to improve our fellowship between the different generations in the church.

As a part of accepting intergenerational collaboration, we should make it known to the youth that their voices matter. In intentionally affirming so, we will actively foster a greater engagement from our youth. When they realize that they are valuable to their family in Christ, they may be emboldened to follow God's calling with even greater passion and commitment.

MY EXPERIENCE

My Youth Experience

One of the things that always bothered me while growing up in youth groups, was when a leader was dismissive of the problems that we faced. Notions like, "Oh, you're just kids, what do you know?" really got under my skin, as such an attitude implied that just because we were young, we did not face any legitimate difficulties or struggles.

Another sentiment that drove me mad was when a leader would "settle" a theological sort of debate by saying "I'm the leader, so therefore I'm right." In addition to being incredibly intellectually dishonest, that approach always struck me as such an easy way out of a conversation; it was a strategy to avoid dealing with any further difficult topics. It also seems to imply that adults have ownership of all knowledge, simply by virtue of being older than their juniors. Of course, while there may be a correlation between life experience and knowledge, that is not an infallible correlation, and there are certainly times in which the older can learn from the younger, for a change. Learning should be mutual, not an exclusively top-down system.

It seems to me that, when adults silence the voices of youth, they reinforce a culture of elitism that runs rampant in many churches today. This is an unfortunate situation; like the ouroboros, it is an unending cycle in which we eat our own tails. In other words, by silencing today's youth, adults establish an elitism that youth, in turn, carry on into their time as tomorrow's adults, wherein they will then silence tomorrow's youth, and the cycle goes on and on. The chain must break eventually.

My Servant Experience

Currently, I take the experiences I had as a youngster and apply them to my service to today's youth. I do my best to affirm their voices, and take what they have to say seriously. They each have something important to bring to the table, and I seek to honor their contributions by giving them a platform, to the best of my ability.

When a young person feels they have something important to say or otherwise contribute to a situation within the church, I try to give them an opportunity to share it. Some may look down on such a system of equality, but I think it is of great importance that we always reaffirm to our youth that their voices matter.

God has given everyone their own perspective, so it makes little sense to me to try and stifle that perspective for some, until they reach some idyllic age of maturity and supreme enlightenment. The truth is, everyone is always growing. Part of a healthy relationship with God is to grow in our knowledge and understanding of

God's ways, and this should never come to a halt with a certain age. If we are all ever-growing, there would seem to be no issue with allowing those to speak who are simply earlier along in their growth. We must remember that young Timothy was encouraged to not let people look down on him because of his age (1 Timothy 4:12). Let us not be the ones who look down on today's young people.

CLOSING QUESTION

In what ways can we elevate the voices of youth within our churches?

8

Hellfire

MY THOUGHTS

IN MANY CONGREGATIONS, THREATS of eternal punishment in hell are a common tactic used to convince people to become Christians. Often times, youth are the primary targets for such threats. The ethically questionable tactic of scaring youth into believing in Christ is not a wise strategy.

One of the primary faults with such tactics is that they are inherently negative. We push people away from a negative (i.e., hellfire) rather than primarily pushing them toward a positive: Jesus. Such tactics are not confined to minor issues, but instead underscore one's entire approach to theology, by revealing how a person understands the very essence of salvation. If salvation is fundamentally regarded as an escape from hell, that is vastly different from regarding salvation primarily as a movement toward Christ.

Imagine that there are two buildings. You are in one of the buildings. Then, you run out of that building and into the other one. Now, you should ask yourself whether you are running from the one building or whether you are running toward the other. If you are indeed running away from the first building, then you are motivated by avoidance, as you are being driven by what you are wanting to get away from. If you are running toward the second building, you are motivated by attraction, because you are being driven by your desire to go toward that second building. One may argue that this is a distinction without a difference, but to raise such an objection would be vastly undervaluing the importance of one's motivations. Motivations fuel everything we do, by definition. Therefore, it stands to reason that the very force that fuels our every action is worthy of extensive contemplation.

Regarding salvation, and our teachings about salvation to our youth, we must examine our hearts and test our motivations. Is salvation really about the human need to avoid being ostensibly burned forever? Or, is salvation actually about the human being's deep longing to be in fellowship and communion with God?

Some would say that the ideal presentation about salvation would be a combination of the two approaches: We ought to run away from hell and run toward Christ. However, even this approach doesn't sit quite right with me. When I look to the New Testament, I struggle to find a clear, unambiguous instance of a potential punishment involving eternal conscious torment in hell being used as a ministry tactic. Instead, the emphasis for ministry is always on following Christ. An approach to salvation that combines both threat and promise does not seem to have a strong biblical precedent. Throughout the New Testament, the promise of Christ is central. To walk with Christ is a decision of attraction instead of aversion.

The use of hellfire threats as a means for somehow bettering our youth can create a culture of fear instead of hope. Fear can be very dangerous. Hope, however, is wonderful and can spur us on to great works for God's kingdom. When we teach students that fear is foundational, we set them up for a dangerous road ahead. Thankfully, though, fear is not foundational for our faith. The three greatest forces which empower our walk with Christ are faith, hope, and love (1 Corinthians 13:13). Fear is nowhere to be found among them.

My Experience

My Youth Experience

In some Christian circles, there are spectacles called "judgment houses." For anyone who is not familiar with such things, picture a haunted house attraction that you can go to around Halloween. Now, instead of running through a house filled with actors pretending to be axe murderers, picture walking through a house or church building filled with various scenes, where actors pretend to die in various ways. From there, imagine going to another scene which depicts a judgement seat in a cloud-filled welkin, where some of the deceased characters get welcomed into eternal bliss, often by actors playing Christ, angels, or the previously deceased family members of the character in question.

After that, you go to the real bread-and-butter scene of these judgment houses: the hell scene. Here, you typically see the deceased characters who had not "accepted Jesus into their hearts." These characters are being ostensibly tortured in a red-lighted room that is supposed to be hell, all the while exclaiming how they were basically good people in life, and so on. From there, you and the other attendees of this spectacle are ushered into another room, where you are pressured to "accept Jesus into your heart" so that you do not have to face a much hotter version of the red-lit room that you just visited. That is a judgment house in a nutshell.

I had the misfortune of attending a type of judgment house event a few times in my middle school days. In fact, youth are often the intended audience for such attractions. The event itself was quite a barn-burner, with a relatively high production value. The wave of people begging to "ask Jesus into their hearts" at the end never disappointed, either.

However, there was always something highly disconcerting about the event. Even in a somewhat unadvanced phase of my theological understanding, the notion of terrifying people into trying to follow Christ did not sit well with me. Even then, I sensed that the emphasis on running away from hell was obfuscating the key notion of running toward Jesus. Later on, I would dive further into the complexities of the whole "asking Jesus into your heart" matter, and how that imperative can sometimes become something different from the call to follow Christ that we find in Scripture. The core notion of avoidance of hell, instead of attraction to Christ, still stands as my biggest concern about such events. Hell-focused gospel presentations, in general, seem counter-productive if not altogether harmful.

My Servant Experience

While I am far-removed from the circles which frequent judgment houses today, I still encounter students who are overly fixated on the notion of hell. Their focus seems to be on that same old wavelength of running from hell as a core tenet of following Christ. This obsession is even more troubling for me now than it was in my younger years. What was then a vague hunch about misaligned priorities regarding hell is now a more developed theological opinion.

I often hear some students say things like, "If I do . . . [a sinful thing], I'm going to burn!" I find this rather upsetting. Even if it is a bit of dark humor that is going over my head, I think it highlights how punitive their understanding of God is, which is a very troubling notion. If they have the idea in their heads that God is waiting for them to slip up, so that they can be flung into eternal flames, then something has gone gravely wrong with their theological understanding.

Because of this situation, my fellow servants and I have to work especially hard to point people toward the pursuit of God, as opposed to the fleeing of hell. We must correct the misconceptions that have been put into the minds of our students by some of the more problematic elements within parts of Christian culture. Our joy is found in the presence of Christ, not in the absence of hell.

CLOSING QUESTION

How can we lovingly admonish our siblings in Christ who promote a misguided, hell-centric understanding of the Gospel?

9

Christians and Nature

MY THOUGHTS

THE WAY A PERSON interacts with the world tells a story. Take nature, for example. Are we users and abusers of nature, or do we coexist peacefully with the natural world? Do we use our resources wisely and equitably, or do we hoard and overindulge ourselves? Questions like these help us to determine exactly how we go about interacting with our environment. Our youth also take note of how we commune with nature.

A prime example, lending insight into our attitude toward the environment, is the way we treat animals. Do we hunt and kill animals for pleasure? Do we run over creatures on the road with our vehicles and only feel indifference? We might ask ourselves, too, whether we are unmoved when a species loses its natural habitat and whether we feel nothing when a species goes extinct. Do we react with compassion when we hear of animals that are slaughtered in cruel and inhumane ways? Let's not forget that animals were created by God, also. This issue may sound trivial to some, but it is far from trivial. Remember, God knows each sparrow that falls to the ground (Matthew 10:29). Even when we don't care for animals, God certainly does. As with all things, it is wiser for us to follow the ways of God than the ways of humankind. The example we set for others by following God's way is of great importance.

If our youth observe us acting in ways that disrespect God's creation, it is possible that they may begin to adopt similar actions as well, which do not measure up to the example set by Christ. Isaiah prophesied that the Suffering Servant will not even do so much as break a bruised reed (Isaiah 42:3). (We know from the Suffering Servant passages in Isaiah, especially the whole of Isaiah 53, that the Servant is Christ.) Gentleness was a notable feature of Jesus, and Jesus Himself said as much (Matthew 11:29), so we should certainly strive for Christlike gentleness.

A gentle approach with youth in the Church can manifest in a number of ways. For instance, we could encourage environmentally friendly practices like recycling. The grand gestures are not always what make the most impact. The little things can help change a person's perspective, which can then lead to lifelong change.

MY EXPERIENCE

My Youth Experience

One thing which really impacted me when I was in high school was a visit to the home of some relatives out in the countryside. Their home had that kind of frontier-like atmosphere to it, relatively secluded in nature. I had loved nature as a small child, but in the years since I had grown distant from it in all its beauty. At that house, though, I rediscovered nature, once again.

One thing which really struck me while there may sound simple, but it resonated with me in a powerful way. They had a compost pile, something I had never actually seen before. A pile in their yard consisted of food that had spoiled, or leftovers like orange peels and other such biodegradable items. The extra foodstuffs, dumped into the pile, did not go to waste. I was fascinated by this process, whereby leftovers were recycled, eventually becoming food for worms and various other creatures. The notion that the things we consume can serve a purpose greater than ourselves was, in some sense, revolutionary to me. It greatly affected the way I view natural resources.

That experience added a new dynamic to the way that I interact with nature around me. By learning to care for our natural resources, I learned a new way in which to honor God. So often, humans are tempted to treat nature as meaningless, consisting simply of resources to use and to discard. At times, I fell into this kind of disregard for our natural environment. However, once I saw my calling to be Christlike as extending to my interactions with the natural world, the paradigm shifted.

My Servant Experience

Many of our youth struggle to see the importance of caring for our natural environment. Surprisingly, speaking of such care can stir up controversy in many church circles. Some will object to talk of preserving nature; since they regard this world as our temporary home, they feel no particular need to care for it.

While this world may be a "temporary home," nevertheless we should not feel free to destroy it. Would the church's environmental skeptics rent a house that they then proceed to demolish? I would certainly hope not. I struggle to understand how the apparently temporary quality of our world could somehow give us permission to exploit it. If we cannot learn to treat this earth with respect, how can we then expect to be treat the "new earth" any differently (Revelation 21:1)?

The value of caring for nature may be difficult for students to latch onto, but I believe this priority is important to instill. For some, such care for nature may come more easily than for others. Since large portions of the western church downplay environmental justice, or otherwise make little mention of it, it is best to be patient with students who are slow to get on board with the task of nurturing the planet. With that being said, we should still nudge them on toward environmental stewardship as best we can. The earth belongs to God (Psalm 24:1). We should treat it as holy, because God is holy.

CLOSING QUESTION

What actions can we take to promote good stewardship of the earth by today's youth?

10

Collective Sin

MY THOUGHTS

THE NOTION OF COLLECTIVE sin is something of which many people are skeptical. However, there is biblical precedent for this idea. One need look no further than Amos 1:3–2:14, where God pronounces judgement upon Israel's neighbors, and then upon Judah and Israel themselves, for the collective sins of their people. Collective sin is a serious danger, and it should not be swept under the rug.

Imagine that there is a sick person in a room full of doctors. The person is dying from a treatable condition, and each of the doctors has the means for a cure. However, suppose that not one of the doctors helps the sick person, and so the illness causes him or her to die. In that case, who is responsible for the person's death? How could one doctor be singled out above all of the rest, especially if they all had the knowledge and means to help, as they do in this hypothetical situation? Some may urge that none can therefore be held responsible, but it seems obvious to me that all of the doctors are responsible and guilty of collective sin.

Picture now a starving person, who is homeless and living on the street right outside of a restaurant. Every day, countless patrons walk by, but none pay the starving person any mind. Any one of them could easily bring the person food from the restaurant, but none do. Eventually, the person succumbs to starvation. Who, then, was responsible for the person's death? Again, it seems apparent that all of the patrons are responsible, as each could have brought the person food, yet none of them did. This group, too, is guilty of collective sin.

Lastly, let's imagine a third person. The driver of a now broken-down car, this person is freezing to death on the side of the road, in the middle of winter. Several motorists pass by, each noticing the person inside the vehicle, each fully aware of the grave weather conditions, and still none of them stop to offer the stranded person any assistance. Before too long, the cold becomes too much and the person passes away. For a third time, we must ask: Who is responsible for this death? For a third time the answer is clear: Everyone who could have done something, but didn't. All of the passing motorists, like the restaurant patrons and the doctors before them, are guilty of collective sin.

Now that we have plainly established that collective sin is real and dangerous, we may look at how to apply this understanding in the context of youth ministry. Our youth ministries can be guilty of collective sin, and when this is the case, the sin should be clearly addressed and repented of, so that our ministry can rectify certain wrongs, both for the sake of the youth and for their ministers and guides.

A common collective sin that takes place within a youth ministry is the exclusion of certain students. In all social groups, cliques may form which shut out certain people. Those shut out can feel cut off from the group as a whole. Dejection or a wholesale abandonment of the church may result. I can say this with confidence, because I was once one of those youngsters who grew greatly dejected over my obvious status as an outsider within my youth group. My dejection even got to the point where I seriously considered giving up on church. Thankfully, God is great in mercy, and Christ's love never abandoned me, the way the rest of the youth group had. Therefore, I can say with conviction that we must be very careful to never ostracize members of our youth groups. Ostracizing can lead to some awful scars, and by abandoning youth, we effectively deviate from the way of Christ.

A group can unwittingly slip into a pattern of collective sin by ignoring the needs in our greater community. In short, where we could be helping, we should be helping, and not helping can lead us into collective sin. For example, let us say that some students are attending school with some of our youth, and these students have rough home lives. Our youth could see and ignore such things, or they can decide to live out Christ's love in the situation, by extending support to their troubled classmates. In shining Christ's light in such away, we show our care and love for the larger community.

If some elderly neighbors of our youth have trouble looking after themselves, and the young people have the choice either to do nothing or to help their elderly neighbors, they can spread Christ's self-giving love and kindness by choosing to help. Again, youth should reach out in love. If we are not fostering an environment for our youth where such acts of kindness and sacrifice are encouraged, we risk slipping into collective sin. In these cases, and in all cases like them that may appear in our different life contexts, we have a choice between being more loving or less loving. At such a crossroads, we should always choose the more loving route. When we do so, we live in a Christlike manner, which is the goal of all of our choices and actions.

It is important that we educate our youth on the nature of collective sin. However, as always, we should not fall into a spiritual fearmongering. Nor ought our discussions harp at length on why we don't want to fall into collective sin. Instead, we should focus on the positive reasons for acting with love and kindness, which then will keep us, in turn, from collective sin. All the good that should be done, and all the Christlike actions that we are able to take, can inspire us to do wonderful things. When we look to Christ as our ultimate example, and live in a way that embodies the love of Christ, we will keep ourselves away from collective sin.

MY EXPERIENCE

My Youth Experience

When I was a member of various youth groups, a certain pattern would often repeat itself. First, students would begin to notice someone in the group who was struggling. Often times, this person was dealing with issues at home or in school. From there, the unspoken question of who would reach out to comfort this person would pass through the group. Most of the time, this question would go unanswered, and the struggler would be left unreached, to face their demons alone. I can only imagine what some of these students went through, and how it was made much worse by none of their peers reaching out to support them.

Unfortunately, there were several times in which the unspoken question came to me, and I let it pass by unanswered. There were other times in which I was the struggler, silently hoping for support which never came. It is baffling to me, in hindsight, how quickly a group can abandon an individual. Tragedy often ensues, and has frequently been disastrous to the faith of many young people.

A youth group falls into collective sin by collectively rejecting someone. When someone needs the love, support, and fellowship of a group, but the group simply leaves the struggler to their own devices, the collective has fallen into sin. It is one thing for the one sheep to wander away from the ninety-nine, but for the ninety-nine to notice the one wandering away, and yet do nothing to help that sheep, is nothing short of abhorrent.

My Servant Experience

In my current role, serving high school students, I have come to believe that this cycle of collective sin is ever-repeating. Just as it happened in my youth group when I was a youth, so it happens still today in the group I serve.

As a ministry servant, I often reach out to those who are excluded, for both their sakes and the sake of the group as a whole. My track record in doing so is far from perfect, but I am working to improve my outreach.

We ought to educate the youth on the dangers of collective sin. Collective sin is not often discussed in certain church circles, but it is a very real and present threat. If more students are informed of this problem, the spiritually mature among them may begin to proactively work against patterns of collective sin forming in their midst. As a servant, there is only so much I can do to prevent these cycles from repeating. The choice is ultimately up to the students. God can and will work on their hearts, which is essential for spiritual transformation and for eliminating collective sin. At some point, however, the students themselves need to take the initiative to avoid collective sin, in conjunction with God's moving in their hearts.

CLOSING QUESTION

What are some helpful ways in which adults can foster an environment for youth that protects against behaviors which lead into collective sin?

11

Exploring Scripture Boldly

MY THOUGHTS

For some, exploring the pages of Scripture can be intimidating. While some of the teachings therein are quite straightforward and clearly practical, other passages can be quite mysterious and hard to make heads or tails of. For every Book of Proverbs there is a Book of Revelation. Sometimes, the clear and the mysterious coexist within the same book, such as in Daniel, where the chapters from one to six consist mostly of historical accounts, while chapters seven through twelve contain visions and prophecy. Sometimes, the perplexing passages in Scripture can be enough to cause some of us to avoid teaching them, while others may opt to teach those passages very lightly and only in passing. Both of those approaches are flawed. The best way to approach Scripture is to dive right in, addressing both mysterious passages and clear.

When we journey through Scripture alongside the youth, we are joining forces on an incredible voyage. No matter the obstacles we face, or the strange waves that rock our boats, we are together, and God is with us. The journey can actually provide us with a tremendous opportunity for bonding. The power of shared experiences creates magic, for instance, in youth camps or mission trips.

The group can experience God in a shared and collective way that unites everyone in a unique bond of fellowship and communion. To journey through Scripture can create such bonds, while the group works together to navigate all the twists and turns throughout the Bible, including narratives, prophecy, and wisdom. This powerful experience can embolden us all and work wonders for building group rapport. We all may grow closer to Christ together, in the process, as a family.

Objections to intense scriptural study may be raised along the lines of fearing that certain passages will prove to be problematic, which could shipwreck our faith. However, I am confident that this fear is misplaced. Such problematic passages must be faced directly; and as a group, it is best to pursue an honest discussion about the difficult points. These group discussions can allow for problematic sections to be worked through as a team. If these passages are avoided in the group context, then I fear they will prove to be much more difficult to sort through when the youth encounter them on an individual basis. There is strength in numbers. Therefore, I believe we should be eager to address even the most difficult passages of Scripture together, in an honest and direct way.

One of the greatest points of Scripture is that, on at least some level, all of it points us toward Jesus. This fact in and of itself is what makes Scripture so priceless. Sometimes people do not make this connection. We can reach a point where we read the Bible in a flat and undynamic way, with the sort of detachment that is more appropriate for reading a dictionary. This attitude is misguided, because Scripture is abundant with richness and depth from cover to cover. When we really dig in and savor that depth, we can experience a wonderful tapestry that is constructed by all of Scripture, and that tapestry has as its center point the person of God revealed in Jesus Christ. This centerpiece highlights the extreme importance of reading through Scripture, so that we can learn to find Christ revealed on every page. This approach should be enough to overpower any reservations or concerns that we may have about a deep and unhindered exploration of the Bible, the sort of exploration that is sure to uncover spiritual gold.

I would be remiss if I were to warn of the dangers of marginalizing Scripture, without also warning of the opposite extreme. Idolization of Scripture should be avoided, to the best of our ability, as such idolization can lead to some dangerous distortions. We should never put Scripture on an equal footing with God. Nothing is equal with God, and anything we attempt to make equal with God instantly becomes an idol. Scripture may be called the word of God, but only Jesus Christ is the Word of God (John 1:1). (Note the capitalization.) Jesus is to be our focus, and because of this, we should never elevate Scripture to the status of God. Scripture is a guide for us, not a god to us, and we should always strive to uphold this distinction.

In short, we should always highlight Scripture's value as a trustworthy guide to Christ Jesus. Let us not be afraid to approach even the most difficult passages, especially if we are doing so as a group which includes our youth, so that we all may grow and learn together. We can develop greatly from such a shared experience. It is best to steer clear of worshipping Scripture in the same way that we worship God. Far from elevating it to the status of idol, let us instead make use of Scripture as an important guide for us in our journey into God's kingdom.

MY EXPERIENCE

My Youth Experience

In middle school, I had a Bible teacher who helped light a fire inside of me for Scripture. Growing up in church, I had already heard most of the Bible stories, but this teacher had a way of bringing the stories to life. God was able to use him to ignite a passion within me for the Bible that has continued to the present day.

There was something special about the way this teacher presented Scripture. It was as if he made stories three-dimensional for me, which had previously only been two-dimensional. One way he did this was by never holding back information. He was always quick to provide a historical, cultural, and textual background for every passage. Up until that point in life, I was not very familiar with such methods.

While I would later encounter other teachers, especially in my recent college learning, who were able to provide a similar depth for Scripture, I will be forever grateful to that particular teacher whom I had all those years ago. God opened my mind to the wonder found within the Biblical texts, thanks in large part to that teacher's guidance.

My Servant Experience

In my current ministry, I have made something of a reputation out of my eagerness to field theological questions. I enjoy the opportunity to intellectually work through questions with students, so that we may both come to a greater knowledge of God. I have held a few question-and-answer sessions with high schoolers, including one where I answered between thirty and forty questions in around forty-five minutes. While I do not necessarily recommend such speed, the session illustrates just how passionate I am about digging into Scripture and theology.

It is a wonderful experience, and sometimes even magical, to be involved in collective studies. Very few things in this world make me feel as though I am exactly where God wants me to be, but being able to answer the theological questions of students is certainly one of those things. I am blessed to have the opportunity to assist students in grasping difficult theological concepts through Scripture.

While I understand how some people within the church as a whole may be hesitant to open the floor to questions from students, for fear of questions which cannot be answered, I am optimistic that an honest avowal of uncertainty (i.e., "I'm not sure") is more fruitful than an avoidance of questions altogether. In most cases, there is at least some answer for every question about Scripture. In the few cases of expository difficulty, we gain an opportunity to lean heavily on faith. Faith helps us through mysteries, but God empowers us to uncover mysteries by seeking answers, so that we may know the way of Christ.

CLOSING QUESTION

How can we best encourage youth to dive into Scripture on their own, so that they may be given a passion for scriptural study?

12

Love and Obedience

MY THOUGHTS

Our youth today do not so much need someone to tell them "who's boss," someone to dominate them because of their rank and status, or someone who is driven to attack them when they've messed up. Youth get enough of that already.

Often times, in youth ministry, leaders will come along who have a passion for discipline. These teachers quickly become known for their stern nature. Savvy students may choose to fall in line, or they may choose to hide how far away from that leader's standards that they are. In other words, students may choose either to abandon their misdeeds, or to simply go underground with those actions. A leader who demands obedience will likely get both of those reactions. The underground response becomes especially prevalent when a leader chooses to enforce obedience before they emphasize love.

If all a student knows to expect from a leader is sternness and incredibly high standards, and this student has no genuine desire to cease the actions that the leader does not approve of, this student may disappear from the ministry altogether. Or, perhaps even more troublingly, this student will learn to bury their difficulties deep underground. The choice to do the latter can have disastrous effects on a young person's faith, as they decide to hide their struggles instead of sharing them, because they are afraid of punishment. When leaders spread fear instead of love, that unfortunate direction will be the path of many students.

Leaders spreading fear will lead to students committed to secrecy. Leaders marked by anger will lead to students who think anger is the only way. Leaders whose calls for obedience are not bookended by love and saturated with compassion will lead to students who see love as the servant of obedience, and do not see obedience as the servant of love. Leaders who lead through intimidation will lead to a generation of resentful students.

So, I must ask: Do we really want our youth to be intimidated by authoritarian personalities? I certainly hope not! It is bad enough that they live in an age where fear is feasted on by society like vultures upon a corpse (Luke 17:37), even though it is society itself which is ever-dying, while our youth still have hope for life! Everywhere we turn, society as we know it is in what would appear to be its death throes, even though I postulate that this "death" of society is only a part of its greater transformation, in the same way that a caterpillar "dies" in the cocoon to become a butterfly. Methods, institutions, and traditions of the old society are crumbling under the pressure of change. With all this change, a brighter future is possible!

So I ask again: Do we really want the oppression of our youth by way of brutish authoritarianism to survive this season of change? The apostle Paul tells us that everyone's workmanship will be tested by fire (1 Corinthians 3:12–15). What really makes us believe that a harsh authoritarianism will survive the flames? I am of the opinion that such menacing behavior will be consumed into nothingness. Intimidating systems are not the way of Jesus Christ.

Jesus tells His followers that we are no longer his servants, but we are instead His friends (John 15:15). Since our Lord has chosen to have a relationship with us that is marked by loving friendship, why do we still choose to define our relationships with youth in terms of authority? Do we want our youth to love God because they obey God? Or, do we want them to obey God because they love God? This distinction may appear minor, but I assure you that it is not. The fuel for our actions should be love. Obedience will flow from love, as we want to please God, whom we love. We cannot be forced to love. We cannot be disciplined into love. Love must come first, and then the obedience will follow.

Given the choice between showing the youth our open arms or our iron fists, what believer in their right minds would choose the latter? Love is the way of Christ! If we do not love, we are nothing (1 Corinthians 13:1–3)! Love is patient, kind, unselfish, unprovoked, with no record kept of wrongs, all-bearing, all-believing, all-hoping, and all-enduring (1 Corinthians 13:4a,5b,7). Now, tell me which of those things is a harsh, human authoritarianism? Indeed, authoritarianism is often impatient, unkind, prone to selfishness and narcissism, easily provoked, obsessed with wrongs, unbearing, unbelieving, hopeless, and unenduring. In that sense, authoritarianism is anti-love, just as fear is the antithesis of love.

Do we love to condemn our youth for their sinful mistakes, or do we serve the Lord who said "Neither do I condemn you..." (John 8:11)?

Do we cast aside our wayward youth when they step out-of-line, or do we serve the God who runs to meet the prodigal children with love (Luke 15:20)?

Do we pour out our anger on youth who we feel slighted by, or do we serve the Messiah, who prayed that even His murderers be forgiven (Luke 23:34)?

The situation before us is clear. We must choose right now, in this very moment, to let our interactions with the youth around us be marked by love, first and foremost. If we want them to be obedient, let us teach them to love. Love is key.

MY EXPERIENCE

My Youth Experience

Of the several youth groups I spent time in while growing up, most of them had at least a few leaders who were of the "break the students down so that they will learn to love Jesus" mentality, to varying degrees. These leaders would typically start their teaching from an instructional standpoint ("Do this, not that"), with the reasons for such instructions to follow. In other words, making us obey them was their first order of business, and molding us into devoted Christ followers was the second.

This instruction by fear brought my theological understanding to an unhealthy place at a relatively young age. God's love for me seemed conditional upon my obedience. Despite being at churches which loudly proclaimed "faith, not works," the notion was instilled in me that communion with God had to be contingent on my behavior as the perfect little Christian. Following such ideas to their logical conclusion, I would often become terrified at the slightest of slip-ups, fearing that all of a sudden God's love would move away from me because of my mistakes. When I wasn't behaving like a good soldier in the army of the Lord, I was taught that a cosmic cold shoulder would be coming my way.

The "boot camp" mentality that hounded me was based on the notion that believers are soldiers in God's army. If a soldier steps out of line, he is punished. That is how soldiering works. However, this ministry philosophy is missing a vital point: We are ambassadors, pointing toward humanity's intended reconciliation with God (2 Corinthians 5:11–21). We are not soldiers, sent on a mission to divide and conquer, and any ministry strategy that aims to treat students as such is misguided in its very premise.

My Servant Experience

Today, I try to guide students on a path of ambassadorship and reconciliation, and not on a path of war. This is not always easy, as some church circles are committed to the "Christian soldier" ethos. When I encounter students from those backgrounds, it can be difficult to demilitarize their theology. To do so generally looks like explaining to them the importance of love and peace in our mindset, and in all our actions.

This direction is key for teaching students how obedience is not the bedrock tenet of Christian faith. Love is. Obedience is important, but true obedience flows from love—not the other way around. Some may deride this as a minor distinction, but I believe it is of the utmost significance.

How we view the centrality of love in our faith informs how we view a great many things, from sin to orthopraxy and to the gospel itself. Love's importance cannot be overstated. As a servant to high school students, it is my responsibility to point them toward the love of Christ as the central foundation of our faith. This foundation informs all of my teaching, just as I hope it goes on to inform all of their actions.

CLOSING QUESTION

How can we ensure that we emphasize obedience in its proper place as an outpouring of love, without presenting it as a prerequisite of love?

13

Christ's Love on Display

MY THOUGHTS

Christ's love goes beyond the limits of our human understanding. We can try to grasp the sheer magnitude of this love, but it ultimately exists beyond the capabilities of our knowledge (Ephesians 3:16–19). Some may try to put human limits on this radical, enduring, sacrificing, and forgiving love, but placing such limits is an unfortunate mistake. No limits can be placed upon the love of Christ. Will we the clay try to restrict the potter's love according to our own understanding (Isaiah 45:9)? We often try to do exactly that, and what's worse is that we often pass these misconceived limitations on to our youth.

We live in the midst of an endless love, a boundless love that encompasses us in every minute of every day. It is to God's love that we owe our very existence, for it is through the love of God that we are able to be united with the Godhead, the source and the very fountain of all our being. All our movements, and indeed our very life, arises from that holy source (Acts 17:28). As we find ourselves in the midst of such a wondrous and powerful force, how can we possibly avoid speaking about it at every opportunity? We cannot possibly avoid sharing with everyone, both young and old, the innumerable joys found in the presence of God's love.

Because of this great reality, we may be inspired to always proclaim to our youth the nature of God's love. If we need an excellent frame of reference for such love (and we do), then we may look no further than the life of Jesus. In the gospel we find the secrets and mysteries of love unveiled and put on full display. For Christ to live an innocent, sinless life, and for Christ to love so radically and unwaveringly, reveals the exceptional magnitude of God's love. For Christ to wash the feet of the disciples, including even Judas his betrayer (John 13:1–17), for Jesus to forgive even those who were his killers (Luke 23:34), and for Christ then to rise from the dead and proclaim not war but peace (John 20:21), all of these instances speak to the radical love that was embodied by the person of Jesus. It is simply impossible to overstate this reality. Christ's love was stopped neither by betrayal nor by death, and this love did not fade in any way with the Resurrection. The love of God revealed in Chris is not a flawed, human sort of love. Instead, this love is greater than the greatest force we could ever imagine. God's love is sacrificial. God's love is unwavering. God's love triumphs over death and the grave. This love extends to lengths beyond what our minds can even begin to grasp.

Poets bear witness to the fact that once a person experiences something of great beauty, that person must then strive to encapsulate that beauty and communicate it to others, so that they, too, may be witnesses to its wonder. Such is our situation when we experience the love of Christ. We can hardly fathom the rich depths of this love, but that should not stop us for even one moment from proclaiming the magnificent nature of this love to all.

In our interactions with youth, the proclamation of love should be our calling card. When they are feeling lost and dejected, Christ's messengers of hope and love should be by their side. By being there for them in love and compassion, we let them know that we are part of something wonderful. We are part of Christ's family, a family that is defined by love in the kingdom of God. This amazing truth can be put on full display for our youth, so that they will be able to see how phenomenal this love is, which can serve as a salve for all of their ailments and a panacea for all of their troubles and worries. Our youth need Christ's love to be magnified to them. This world can often be a difficult, dangerous, and unforgiving place, but we know that in Christ, we have overcome the world, just as Jesus has (John 16:33).

Humanity tries all too often to overcome through our own strength. We create myths which lead us to believe that we can conquer anything. Many have tried to do just that. By accepting the myths of self-sufficiency that humanity has created, a person begins to believe that they are able to will their way into overcoming the world. However, this is a fool's errand. The world is not overcome through human ingenuity, calculations, or dominance. The world is not overcome through swords, guns, or bombs. The world is overcome through the matchless love of God revealed in Christ Jesus.

MY EXPERIENCE

My Youth Experience

I spent some time in a youth group program that was well-known by the churchgoers in the area as being especially punitive and legalistic. Standards there were everything. A particular attire was expected, particular behavior, and so on. We would often pledge allegiance to the American flag and the "Christian flag," as well as to the Bible. (Strangely, I do not remember there being a pledge of allegiance to Jesus.)

Christ's love was hardly a focal point of the teachings in this group. If there had been an active count going for the number of times that various words like "love," "holiness," and "law" were mentioned in any given service, "love" would be the odds-on favorite to finish last, each and every time. Of course, that is not to say that holiness means nothing, or that God's law means nothing. By no means! However, it is unfortunate when the love of Christ is forced into a subordinate role in ostensibly Christian teaching.

In truth, Christ's love is central to the gospel. Therefore, teachers marginalizing love is less than ideal. Such a misalignment of priorities is what I was exposed to in that particular group.

This experience of mine is hardly unique, and there are many youth groups out there which find themselves caught up in a heavy wave of loveless legalism. If we do not love, we are nothing (1 Corinthians 13:2). That is an important truth to keep in mind.

My Servant Experience

Today, I take those lessons that I learned in my youth group days and I try to ensure that my setting and context never become bereft of love. Thankfully, I am blessed to serve in a ministry that consistently emphasizes the love of Christ. Nonetheless, I believe it is important to be vigilant, and ensure that our message remains permeated with love.

Throughout my ministry service, I sometimes encounter students who come from legalistic church backgrounds. Having been in their shoes before, I definitely empathize with their situation. With such students, I work on teaching how Scripture clearly and consistently points to the love of God. This unmistakable pattern throughout the Bible is shrouded by some legalistic thinkers and preachers. Problematic teachings leave a lasting impact on theological understandings, causing many young people to stumble.

Followers of Christ can show others how central love is to our faith by living that principle out. We must live our lives in a manner defined by our love for God and those around us. When we show that our faith is not driven by a rigid box-checking, but instead by love, we begin to rewrite the script. Those trapped in legalism discover a better way, a way which follows in the blessed footsteps of Jesus Christ, the perfecter of love.

CLOSING QUESTION

What measures can we take to ensure that love never gets lost in our teaching?

14

Passion for Our Calling

MY THOUGHTS

WE ARE CALLED TO be citizens of God's kingdom. This responsibility may fill us with joy, while also inspiring determination to face any obstacle which life may throw our way. If we are driven to share this good news with our youth, as well, we may then let them know the great work of which they are a part.

People often marvel at the grandeur of the universe, and with good reason. It is often quite a humbling experience, for we as humans to realize how tiny we are in relation to the magnificent universe. We are then able to see ourselves as minor pieces in a cosmic system. The sheer magnitude of this realization is enough for many to be convinced to let go of their pride, and understandably so. However, we who follow Christ realize that we are part of something far grander and more expansive than the known universe in all its vastness. The kingdom of God goes beyond the breadth of the known universe, and encompasses all worlds known and unknown. What's more is that, unlike our relative insignificance in the known universe, we have an important and honorable role to play in the cosmic kingdom of God. We are to be the bearers of God's image. This task is a sacred blessing, the significance of which cannot be overstated.

Another wonderful facet of our role in God's kingdom is that we do not take our instructions from afar, hoping only distantly to embody them as best we can. No, we have God in our very midst, thanks to the dwelling of God's Spirit among us, the very same Spirit that Jesus promised, the Spirit that will empower us to do even greater works than Jesus did during the incarnate ministry (John 14:12). The very power and presence of God is with us through the Spirit. We are the recipients of blessing upon blessing because of this wonderful reality.

Our call to action can be like none other, for both ourselves and the youth among us. We are citizens of God's kingdom, and we are united to God in such a way that can only be described as mystical. When we really think about it, how can words even capture the nature of this union? We are part of God's kingdom, and God's kingdom is alive through the Holy Spirit within us. Our union with God can inspire a virtually infinite number of praises, ideas, movements, and masterpieces from our youth. If we are able to successfully point them toward this grand, cosmic plan of God's, which is revealed to us in Christ, great things will be done. If we can show them how we are part of God's kingdom, ambassadors for Christ to all of God's creation, then we will be fruitful in our ministries and in our service.

Let us always remember to urge our youth onward into the kingdom. We can help them to see the wonder in the mystical union that we share with God. When we truly see the importance of such things, all the cares of our lives will melt away in comparison. Youth often struggle to escape the pressures and distractions of their world, and this is understandable, because the world can be a very difficult place to traverse. However, the truth of God's kingdom holds within it the love, the beauty, the wisdom, and the wonder needed to heal our wounds. The balm of Gilead is found in the arms of Christ, our healer (Jeremiah 8:22). Jesus is our righteousness. We are called to run into the arms of love, and to spread the love of Jesus to all people, all places, and all things! This calling should be with us, like a warming, illuminating flame in the bitter winters and dead of night.

Going forward, with our eyes fixed on God's Kingdom, let's all work together, both young and old alike, to spread this kingdom on earth as it is in heaven (Matthew 6:10). May we share the love of Christ Jesus with one another, and with the whole world.

MY EXPERIENCE

My Youth Experience

Despite growing up in church, the fire within me remained cold for quite a long time. There were flashes of heat here and there, but for the most part, any significant flames remained dormant. While my brain often absorbed things like a sponge, my heart lagged behind. There was a door within me, but it seemed closed for a period of time.

At some point, God flung that door wide open. Passion engulfed me like never before. Things that had seemed dead and lifeless, and bare like mere words on a page, all of a sudden came to life right before my eyes. The stagnant embers became a dynamic fire. The withered winter tree sprung forth vibrant leaves of springtime. My apathetic slumber ended and an energized sprinting began. My faith led me in time to marathon contests of endurance.

If I could go back in time, I would never have imagined that I would be where I am today. I would never have thought that God would call me to follow Christ, yet here I am. It is an amazing gift that I have been given, and God gives this gift freely to all who seek after Christ. I am forever grateful that I have now become so blessed as to know God.

My Servant Experience

I know this passion can fill the hearts of anyone. That is why, in my interactions with youth, I hope to bring them all closer to Jesus. Living out the way of Christ is not always easy in this life, and perhaps in some sense it is not supposed to be, but the journey is worthy of all sacrifices.

Because of all this, I experience the urge to work tirelessly, so that those wandering far away may be brought close to God. May the fire of passion consume each of us from within like a blaze amid the winter snow. The fire used to glow yesterday, it is glowing today, and it will glow again, tomorrow.

May all experience God's presence within them like a fire held in their hearts and in their bones (Jeremiah 20:9). May our youth be ever-impassioned to share Christ's love with others. Amen!

CLOSING QUESTION

As the fire ignites within us, what shall we do with it?

Appendix
The Ministry Ship and the Sea

As I said in the introduction, I presently find myself perched upon the side of the ministry ship. While I am not yet considered a "legitimate" crewman aboard this vessel, the shore is far behind me. There is no turning back. Although my location on the side of the boat is precarious, it gives me a view much different than that seen by some of the crew on deck. I can see the sea in all its vastness and I can see many of the other boats upon the waves.

We are not far from a great many smaller vessels, which are barely remaining afloat. Shall we stop the ministry ship to offer them assistance? I certainly hope so, but too often it seems as though some ministry ships will only stop for yachts.

Jesus was not afraid to leave the comfort of the ministry ship behind. Christ did not hesitate to assist the smaller vessels, and help guide them to safety. I should do likewise. We should all do likewise.

www.ingramcontent.com/pod-product-compliance
Lightning Source LLC
Chambersburg PA
CBHW051705090426
42736CB00013B/2545